THE OWL AND THE PUSSY CAT WENT TO SEA

And Other Nonsense Verse

Edited by ALICE MILLS

Premier

Contents

Contents

The Owl and
the Pussy-Cat

I

The Owl and the Pussy-Cat went to sea
In a beautiful pea-green boat,
They took some honey, and plenty of
    money,
Wrapped up in a five-pound note.
The Owl looked up to the stars above,
And sang to a small guitar,
"O lovely Pussy! O Pussy, my love,
"What a beautiful Pussy you are,
"You are,
"You are!
"What a beautiful Pussy you are!"

II

Pussy said to the Owl, "You elegant fowl!

"How charmingly sweet you sing!

"O let us be married! too long we have
tarried:

"But what shall we do for a ring?"

They sailed away for a year and a day,

To the land where the Bong-tree grows,

And there in a wood a Piggy-wig stood,

With a ring at the end of his nose,

His nose,

His nose,

With a ring at the end of his nose.

III

"Dear Pig, are you willing to sell for one
    shilling,
"Your ring?" Said the Piggy, "I will."
So they took it away, and were married
    next day,
By the Turkey who lives on the hill.

They dined on mince, and slices of quince,
Which they ate with a runcible spoon;
And hand in hand, on the edge of the sand,
They danced by the light of the moon,
The moon,
The moon,
They danced by the light of the moon.

There was a Young Lady of Bute,

Who played on a silver-gilt flute;

She played several jigs,

To her uncle's white pigs,

That amusing Young Lady of Bute.

There was an Old Man of Berlin,

Whose form was uncommonly thin;

Till he once, by mistake,

Was mixed up in a cake,

So they baked that Old Man of
    Berlin.

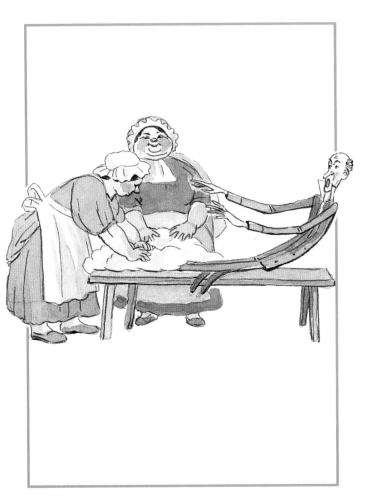

There was an Old Person of Dutton,
Whose head was as small as a button;
So, to make it look big,
He purchased a wig,
And rapidly rushed about Dutton.

There was an Old Man in a Barge,
Whose nose was exceedingly large;
But in fishing by night,
It supported a light,
Which helped that Old Man in a
    Barge.

21

The Pobble who has no Toes

I

The Pobble who has no toes
Had once as many as we;
When they said, "Some day you may lose
  them all,"
He replied—"Fish fiddle de-dee!"
And his Aunt Jobiska made him drink,
Lavender water tinged with pink,
For she said, "The world in general knows
"There's nothing so good for a Pobble's
  toes!"

II

The Pobble who has no toes
Swam across the Bristol Channel;
But before he set out he wrapped his nose,
In a piece of scarlet flannel.
For his Aunt Jobiska said, "No harm
"Can come to his toes if his nose is warm;
"And it's perfectly known that a Pobble's
    toes,
"Are safe—provided he minds his nose."

III

The Pobble swam fast and well,
And when boats or ships came near him,
He tinkledy-binkledy-winkled a bell,
So that all the world could
    hear him.

And all the Sailors and Admirals cried,
When they saw him nearing the further
  side—
"He has gone to fish, for his Aunt
  Jobiska's,
    "Runcible Cat with crimson
  whiskers!"

IV

But before he touched the shore,
The shore of the Bristol Channel,
A sea-green Porpoise carried away
His wrapper of scarlet flannel.
And when he came to observe his feet,
Formerly garnished with toes so neat,
His face at once became forlorn
On perceiving that all his toes were gone!

V

And nobody ever knew
From that dark day to the present,
Whoso had taken the Pobble's toes,
In a manner so far from pleasant.
Whether the shrimps or crawfish gray,
Or crafty Mermaids stole them away—
Nobody knew; and nobody knows,
How the Pobble was robbed of his twice
    five toes!

VI

The Pobble who has no toes
Was placed in a friendly Bark,
And they rowed him back, and carried
    him up,
To his Aunt Jobiska's park.
And she made him a feast at his earnest
    wish

Of eggs and buttercups fried with fish—
And she said—"It's a fact the whole world
knows,
"That Pobbles are happier without their
toes."

There was a Young Lady of Welling,
Whose praise all the world was
    a-telling;
She played on a harp,
And caught several carp,
That accomplished Young Lady
    of Welling.

There was an Old Man with a
    beard,
Who said, "It is just as I feared!—
Two Owls and a Hen,
Four Larks and a Wren,
Have all built their nests in my
    beard!"

There was an Old Man of Aosta,
Who possessed a large cow, but he
   lost her;
But they said, "Don't you see,
She has rushed up a tree?
You invidious Old Man of Aosta!"

There was a Young Person of Bantry,

Who frequently slept in the pantry;

When disturbed by the mice,

She appeased them with rice,

That judicious Young Person of Bantry.

The Jumblies

I

They went to sea in a Sieve, they did,
In a Sieve they went to sea:
In spite of all their friends could say,
On a winter's morn, on a stormy day,
In a Sieve they went to sea!
And when the Sieve turned round and round,
And every one cried, "You'll all be drowned!"
They called aloud, "Our Sieve ain't big,
"But we don't care a button! we don't care
   a fig!
"In a Sieve we'll go to sea!"
Far and few, far and few,
Are the lands where the Jumblies live;
Their heads are green, and their hands are blue,
And they went to sea in a Sieve.

II

They sailed away in a Sieve, they did,
In a Sieve they sailed so fast,
With only a beautiful pea-green veil
Tied with a riband by way of a sail,
To a small tobacco-pipe mast;
And every one said, who saw them go,
"O won't they be soon upset, you know!
"For the sky is dark, and the voyage is long,
"And happen what may, it's extremely wrong
"In a Sieve to sail so fast!"
Far and few, far and few,
Are the lands where the Jumblies live;
Their heads are green, and their hands are
    blue,
And they went to sea in a Sieve.

III

The water it soon came in, it did,

The water it soon came in;

So to keep them dry, they wrapped their feet

In a pinky paper all folded neat,

And they fastened it down with a pin.

And they passed the night in a crockery-jar,

And each of them said, "How wise we are!

"Though the sky be dark, and the voyage be
    long,

"Yet we never can think we were rash or
    wrong,

"While round in our Sieve we spin!"

Far and few, far and few,

Are the lands where the Jumblies live;

Their heads are green, and their hands are
    blue,

And they went to sea in a Sieve.

IV

And all night long they sailed away;
And when the sun went down,
They whistled and warbled a moony song
To the echoing sound of a coppery gong,
In the shade of the mountains brown.
"O Timballo! How happy we are,
"When we live in a sieve and a crockery-jar.
"And all night long in the moonlight pale,
"We sail away with a pea-green sail,
"In the shade of the mountains brown!"
Far and few, far and few,
Are the lands where the Jumblies live;
Their heads are green, and their hands are
    blue
And they went to sea in a Sieve.

V

They sailed to the Western Sea, they did,
To a land all covered with trees,
And they bought an Owl, and a useful Cart,
And a pound of Rice, and a Cranberry Tart,
And a hive of silvery bees.
And they bought a Pig, and some green
    Jackdaws,
And a lovely Monkey with lollipop paws,
And forty bottles of Ring-Bo-Ree,
And no end of Stilton Cheese.
Far and few, far and few,
Are the lands where the Jumblies live;
Their heads are green, and their hands are
    blue,
And they went to sea in a Sieve.

VI

And in twenty years they all came back,
In twenty years or more,
And every one said, "How tall they've grown!

For they've been to the Lakes, and the Terrible
    Zone,
"And the hills of the Chankly Bore;"
And they drank their health, and gave them
    a feast
Of dumplings made of beautiful yeast;
And every one said, "If we only live,
"We too will go to sea in a Sieve,—
"To the hills of the Chankly Bore!"
Far and few, far and few,
Are the lands where the Jumblies live;
Their heads are green,
    and their hands
    are blue,
And they went to
    sea in a Sieve.

There was an Old Lady whose folly,

Induced her to sit in a holly;

Whereupon, by a thorn,

Her dress being torn,

She quickly became melancholy.

There was a Young Lady of Norway,

Who casually sat in a doorway;

When the door squeezed her flat,

She exclaimed, "What of that?"

This courageous Young Lady of

Norway.

There was an Old Man with a flute,
A "sarpint" ran into his boot;
But he played day and night,
Till the "sarpint" took flight,
And avoided that man with a flute.

There was an Old Man of Blackheath,

Whose head was adorned with a Wreath,

Of lobsters and spice,

Pickled onions and mice,

That uncommon Old Man of Blackheath.

The Dong with a
Luminous Nose

∾

When awful darkness and silence reign
Over the great Gromboolian plain,
Through the long, long wintry nights;—
When the angry breakers roar
As they bear on the rocky shore;—
When Storm-clouds brood on the towering
    heights
Of the Hills of the Chankly Bore:—

Then, through the vast and gloomy dark,
There moves what seems a fiery spark,
A lonely spark with silvery rays
Piercing the coal-black night,—
A meteor strange and bright:—
Hither and thither the vision strays,
A single lurid light.

Slowly it wanders,—pauses,—creeps,—
Anon it sparkles,—flashes and leaps;
And ever as onward it gleaming goes
A light on the Bong-tree stems it throws.
And those who watch at that midnight hour
From Hall or Terrace, or lofty Tower,
Cry, as the wild light passes along,—

"The Dong!—the Dong!
"The wandering Dong
    through the forest goes!
"The Dong! the Dong!
"The Dong with a luminous
    Nose!"

Long years ago
The Dong was happy and gay,
Till he fell in love with a Jumbly Girl
Who came to those shores one day.
For the Jumblies came in a Sieve, they did,—
Landing at eve near the Zemmery Fidd
Where the Oblong Oysters grow,
And the rocks are smooth and gray.
And all the woods and the valleys rang
With the Chorus they daily and nightly sang,—
"Far and few, far and few,
Are the lands where the Jumblies live;
Their heads are green, and their hands are
  blue,
And they went to sea in a Sieve."

Happily, happily passed those days!
While the cheerful Jumblies staid;
They danced in circlets all night long,
To the plaintive pipe of the lively Dong,

In moonlight, shine, or shade.
For day and night he was always there
By the side of the Jumbly Girl so fair,
With her sky-blue hands, and her sea-green
  hair,
Till the morning came of that hateful day
When the Jumblies sailed in their Sieve away,
And the Dong was left on the cruel shore

Gazing—gazing for evermore,—
Ever keeping his weary eyes on
That pea-green sail on the far horizon,—
Singing the Jumbly Chorus still
As he sat all day on the grassy hill,—
"Far and few, far and few,
Are the lands where the Jumblies live;
Their heads are green, and their hands are
    blue,
And they went to sea in a Sieve."

But when the sun was low in the West,
The Dong arose and said,—
"What little sense I once possessed
"Has quite gone out of my head!"
And since that day he wanders still
By lake and forest, marsh and hill,
Singing—"O somewhere, in valley or plain
"Might I find my Jumbly Girl again!
"For ever I'll seek by lake and shore
"Till I find my Jumbly Girl once more!"

Playing a pipe with silvery squeaks,
Since then his Jumbly Girl he seeks,
And because by night he could not see,
He gathered the bark of the Twangum Tree
On the flowery plain that grows.
And he wove him a wondrous Nose,—
A Nose as strange as a Nose could be!
Of vast proportions and painted red,
And tied with cords to the back of his head.
—In a hollow rounded space it ended
With a luminous lamp
    within suspended
All fenced about
With a bandage stout
To prevent the wind
    from blowing it
    out;—
And with holes all round
    to send the light,
In gleaming rays on the
    dismal night.

And now each night, and all night long,
Over those plains still roams the Dong;
And above the wail of the Chimp and Snipe
You may hear the squeak of his plaintive pipe
While ever he seeks, but seeks in vain
To meet with his Jumbly Girl again;
Lonely and wild—all night he goes,—
The Dong with a luminous Nose!
And all who watch at the midnight hour,
From Hall or Terrace, or lofty Tower,
Cry, as they trace the Meteor bright,
Moving along through the dreary night,—
"This is the hour when forth he goes,
"The Dong with a luminous Nose!
"Yonder—over the plain he goes;
"He goes!
"He goes;
"The Dong with a luminous Nose!"

There was a Young Lady whose
    nose,
Was so long that it reached to her
    toes;
So she hired an old lady,
Whose conduct was steady,
To carry that wonderful nose.

There was an Old Man of Moldavia,

Who had the most curious behaviour;

For while he was able,

He slept on a table,

That funny Old Man of Moldavia.

There was an Old Person of Anerley,
Whose conduct was strange and
    unmannerly;
He rushed down the Strand,
With a pig in each hand,
But returned in the evening to
    Anerley.

There was an Old Person of Pinner,

As thin as a lathe if not thinner;

They dressed him in white,

And roll'd him up tight,

That elastic Old Person of Pinner.

The Duck and
the Kangaroo

I

Said the Duck to the Kangaroo,
"Good gracious! how you hop!
"Over the fields and the water too,
"As if you never would stop!
"My life is a bore in this nasty pond,
"And I long to go out in the world
      beyond!
"I wish I could hop like you!"
Said the Duck to the Kangaroo.

II

"Please give me a ride on your back!"
Said the Duck to the Kangaroo.
"I would sit quite still, and say nothing
    but 'Quack',
"The whole of the long day through!
"And we'd go to the Dee, and the Jelly
    Bo Lee,
"Over the land, and over
    the sea—
"Please take me a ride! O do!"
Said the Duck to the Kangaroo.

III

Said the Kangaroo to the Duck,

"This requires some little reflection;

"Perhaps on the whole it might bring me
    luck,

"And there seems but one objection,

"Which is, if you'll let me speak so bold,

"Your feet are unpleasantly wet and cold,

"And would probably give me the roo—

"Matiz!" said the Kangaroo.

IV

Said the Duck, "As I sat on the rocks,

"I have thought over that completely,

"And I bought four pairs of worsted socks,

"Which fit my web-feet neatly.

"And to keep out the cold I've bought a
    cloak,
"And every day a
    cigar I'll smoke,
"All to follow my
    own dear true
"Love of a
    Kangaroo!"

V

Said the Kangaroo, "I'm ready!

"All in the moonlight pale,

"But to balance me well, dear Duck, sit
steady!

"And quite at the end of my tail!"

So away they went with a hop and a
bound,

And they hopped the whole world three
times round;

And who so happy—O who,

As the Duck and the Kangaroo?

There was an Old Man of Coblenz,
The length of whose legs was
    immense;
He went with one prance,
From Turkey to France,
That surprising Old Man of Coblenz.

There was a Young Lady whose
    bonnet
Came untied when the birds sat
    upon it;
But she said, "I don't care!
All the birds in the air
Are welcome to sit on my bonnet!

There was an Old Man on a hill,
Who seldom, if ever, stood still;
He ran up and down
In his grandmother's gown,
Which adorned that Old Man on
a hill.

The Table and the Chair

I

Said the Table to the Chair,
"You can hardly be aware
"How I suffer from the heat,
"And from chilblains on my feet!
"If we took a little walk,
"We might have a little talk!
"Pray let us take the air!"
Said the Table to the Chair.

II

Said the Chair unto the Table,
"Now you *know* we are not able!
"How foolishly you talk,
"When you know we *cannot* walk!"
Said the Table with a sigh,
"It can do no harm to try;
"I've as many legs as you,
"Why can't we walk on two?"

III

So they both went slowly down,
And walked about the town
With a cheerful bumpy sound,
As they toddled round and round.
And everybody cried,
As they hastened to their side,
"See! the Table and the Chair
"Have come out to take the air!"

IV

But in going down an ally,
To a castle in the valley,
They completely lost their way,
And wandered all the day.
Till, to see them safely back,
They paid a Ducky-quack,
And a Beetle, and a Mouse,
Who took them to their house.

V

Then they whispered to each other,
"O delightful little brother!
"What a lovely walk we've taken!
"Let us dine on Beans and Bacon!"
So the Ducky and the leetle
Browny-Mousy and the Beetle,
Dined, and danced upon their heads,
Till they toddled to their beds.

There was an Old Man of Nepaul,
From his horse had a terrible fall;
But, though split quite in two,
With some very strong glue,
They mended that Man of Nepaul.

There was a Young Lady whose
    chin,
Resembled the point of a pin;
So she had it made sharp,
And purchased a harp,
And played several tunes with her
    chin.

There was an Old Man of Melrose,
Who walked on the tips of his toes;
But they said, "It ain't pleasant,
To see you at present,
You stupid Old Man of Melrose."

Random House Australia Pty Ltd
20 Alfred Street, Milsons Point NSW 2061

Sydney New York Toronto London Auckland Johannesburg and
agencies throughout the world

First published in 1998
This collection, text and illustrations copyright © Random House
Australia Pty Ltd

The Random House children's treasury gift set.

ISBN 0 09 1836107.

1. Children's poetry. 2. Nonsense literature. 3. Nonsense verses.
4 Tongue twisters.

808.899282

Publisher: Gordon Cheers
Publishing Co-ordinator: Sarah Sherlock
Managing Editor: Marie-Louise Taylor
Designer: Stan Lamond
Typesetter: Dee Rogers

Film separation by Pica Colour Separation Overseas Pte Ltd,
Singapore
Printed in Indonesia

Acknowledgements

All illustrations by Lialia and Valentin Varetsa.
All text by Edward Lear.